Sound

by Grace Hansen

Abdo Kids Jumbo is an Imprint of Abdo Kids
abdopublishing.com

abdopublishing.com

Published by Abdo Kids, a division of ABDO, P.O. Box 398166, Minneapolis, Minnesota 55439.

Abdo Kids Jumbo™ is a trademark and logo of Abdo Kids.

052018

092018

Photo Credits: iStock, Science Source, Shutterstock

Production Contributors: Teddy Borth, Jennie Forsberg, Grace Hansen

Design Contributors: Dorothy Toth, Laura Mitchell

Library of Congress Control Number: 2017960574

Publisher's Cataloging-in-Publication Data

Names: Hansen, Grace, author.

Title: Sound / by Grace Hansen.

Description: Minneapolis, Minnesota : Abdo Kids, 2019. | Series: Beginning science | Includes glossary, index and online resources (page 24).

Identifiers: ISBN 9781532108129 (lib.bdg.) | ISBN 9781532109102 (ebook) | ISBN 9781532109591 (Read-to-me ebook)

Subjects: LCSH: Sound--Juvenile literature. | Acoustics--Juvenile literature.

Classification: DDC 534--dc23

Table of Contents

What Is Sound?

Sound is a wave! Sound waves can travel through **fluids** and solids.

Sound waves are **longitudinal waves**. Particles in the air **vibrate** in the same direction as the wave travels.

F.D.
N.Y.

When the sound waves travel, particles in the air **vibrate**. Then those particles vibrate the air around them. This keeps happening, causing sound waves to spread outward.

Sound waves can also be called pressure waves. Sound waves cause some particles in the air to bunch up. Other particles spread out.

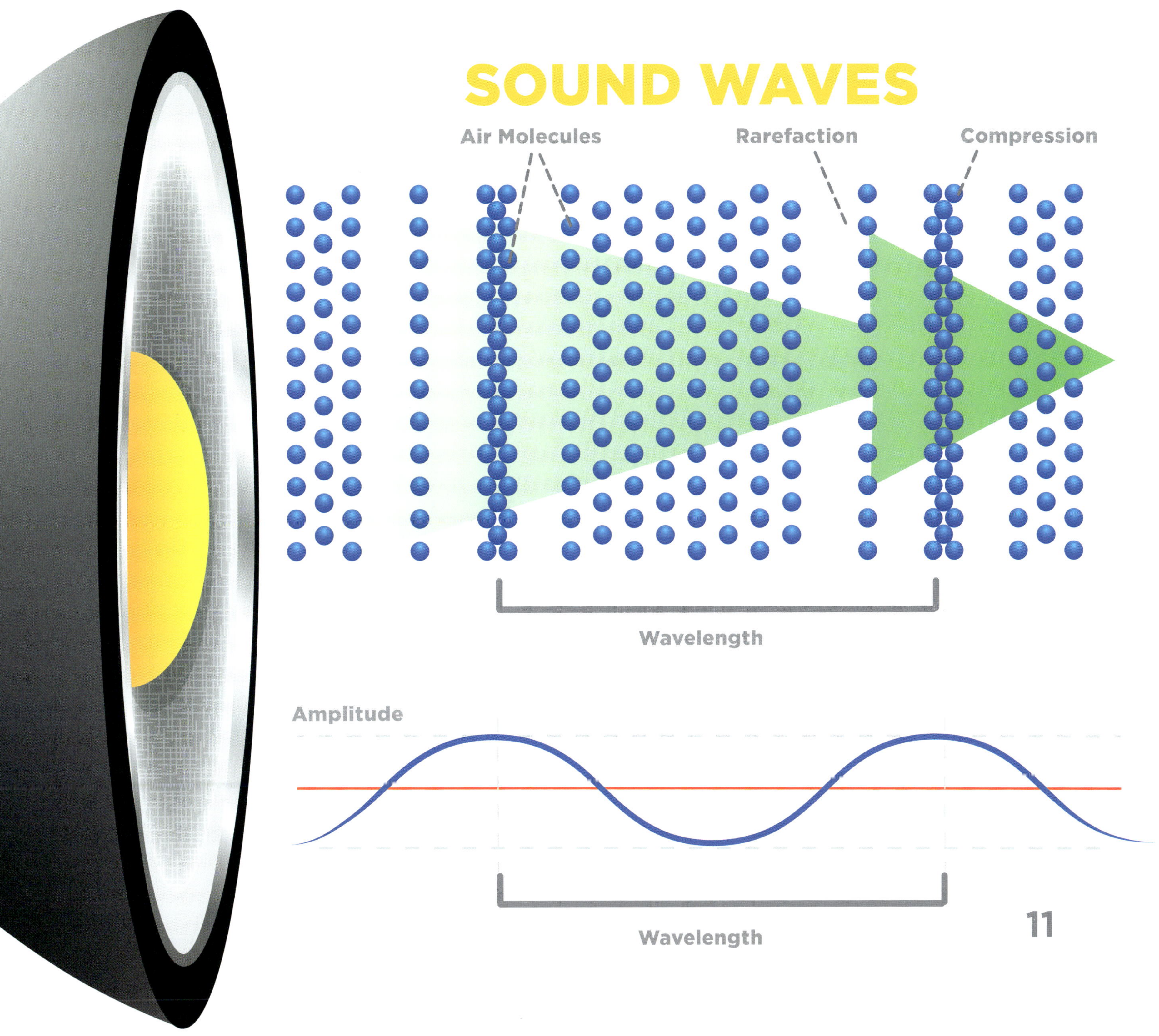
SOUND WAVES
Air Molecules
Rarefaction
Compression
Wavelength
Amplitude
Wavelength

You can hear because pressure waves hit your eardrums. They make your eardrums **vibrate**. Your brain **interprets** the vibrations as sound.

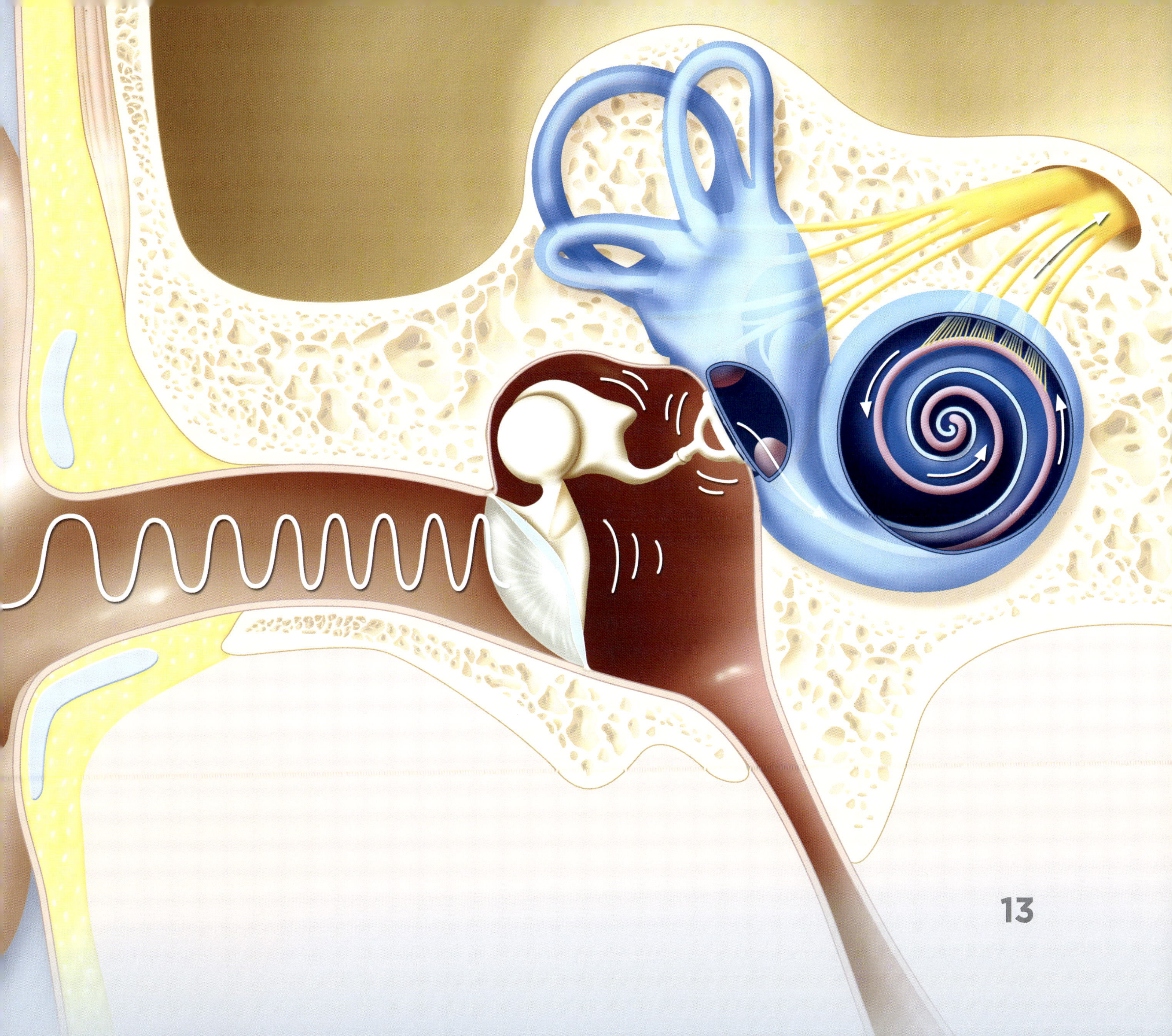

Pitch & Volume

Not all sounds are the same. **Pitch** can be high or low. It matches the **frequency** of the wave.

Air that **vibrates** faster has a higher **pitch**. A whistle makes a high-pitched sound. Air that vibrates slower has a lower pitch. A tuba makes a low-pitched sound.

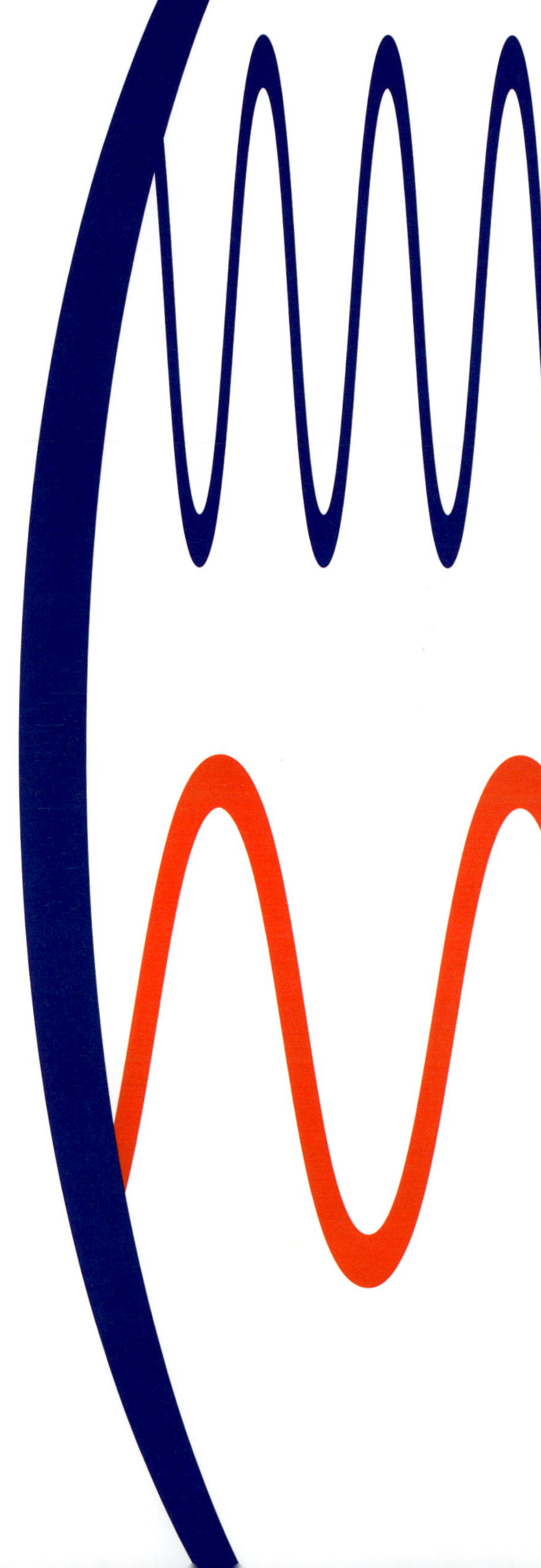

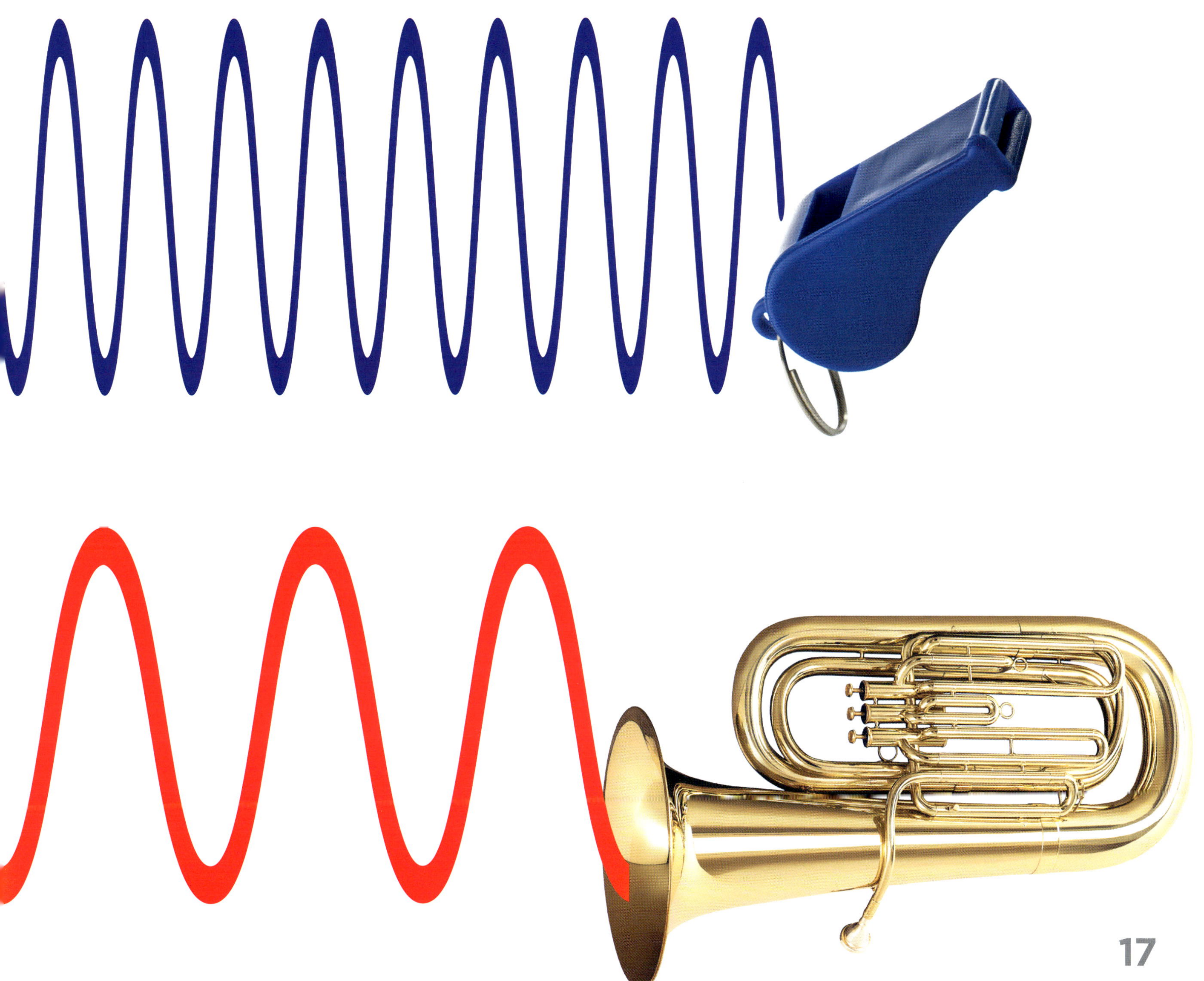

The higher the **intensity** of a sound, the louder it is. A decibel is a unit used to measure the intensity of a sound.

A whisper is a faint sound. It is about 30 decibels. A police siren is extremely loud. It is about 120 decibels.

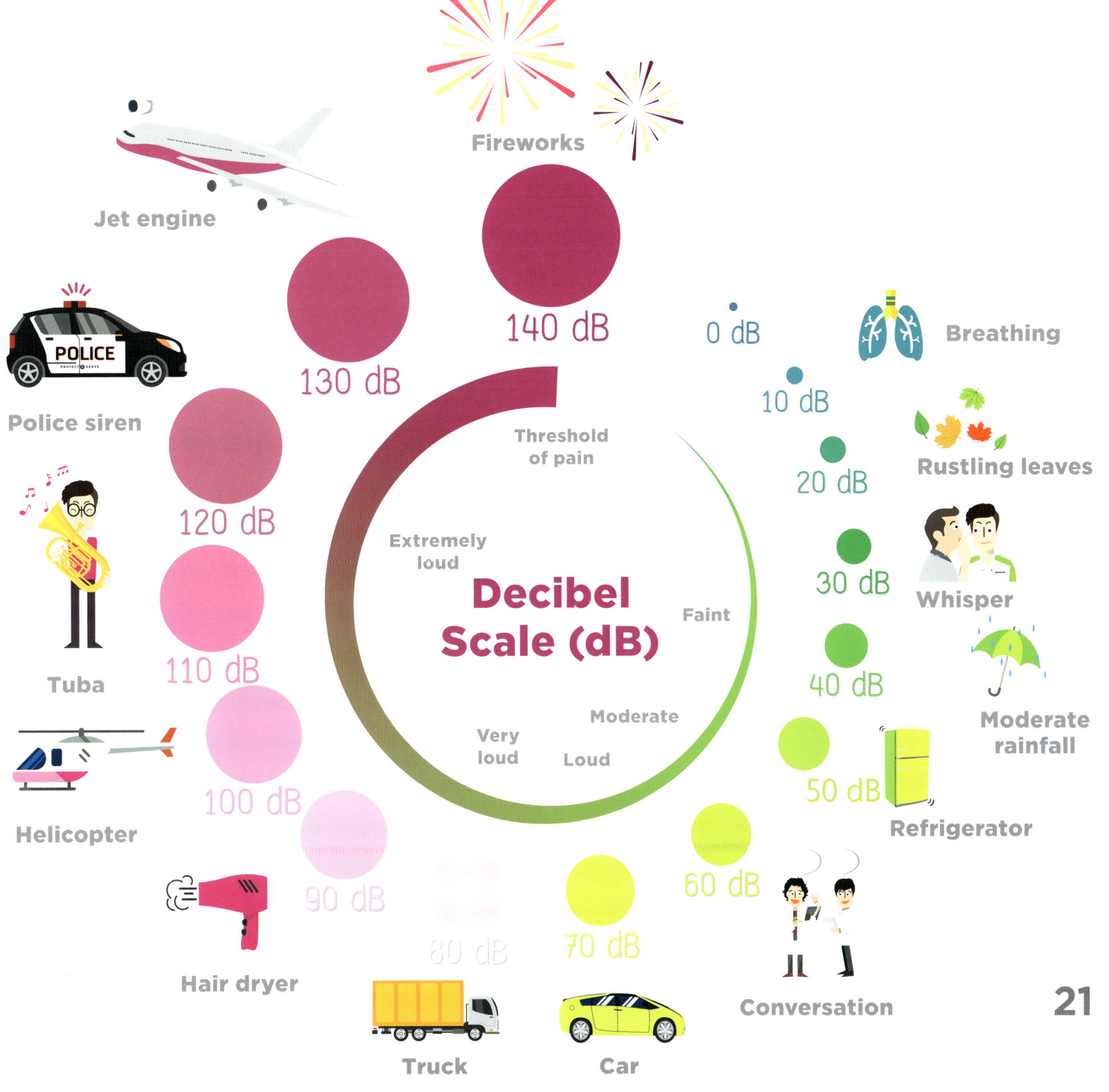
Fireworks
Jet engine
140 dB
130 dB
Police siren
POLICE
120 dB
Tuba
110 dB
Helicopter
100 dB
Hair dryer
90 dB
80 dB
Truck
70 dB
Car
60 dB
Conversation
50 dB
Refrigerator
40 dB
Moderate rainfall
30 dB
Whisper
20 dB
Rustling leaves
10 dB
0 dB
Breathing
Threshold of pain
Extremely loud
Decibel Scale (dB)
Faint
Moderate
Very loud
Loud

Let's Review!

- Sound is an energy wave.
- Sound waves are longitudinal. Particles in the air **vibrate** in the same direction that the wave is traveling.
- Particles in a sound wave bunch up and spread out as they travel. This is called a pressure wave.
- A decibel is a unit used to measure the loudness of a sound.

Glossary

fluid – a liquid or gas. A fluid flows easily and takes the shape of the container that holds it. Water and air are fluids.

frequency – the number of energy waves that pass a certain point in a certain time period.

intensity – the power carried by sound waves.

interprets – understands.

longitudinal wave – a wave which moves particles in the direction of the wave motion.

pitch – the high or low quality of a sound.

vibrate – to move back and forth very rapidly and steadily.

Index

Visit abdokids.com and use this code to access crafts, games, videos, and more!